Date: 9/18/12

J 597.48 DUN
Dunn, Mary R.
Piranhas /

South American Animals

Piranhas

by Mary R. Dunn   Gail Saunders-Smith, PhD, Consulting Editor

Consultant: Brooke Weinstein, Biologist II
Steinhart Aquarium
California Academy of Sciences

CAPSTONE PRESS
a capstone imprint

Pebble Plus is published by Capstone Press,
1710 Roe Crest Drive, North Mankato, Minnesota 56003.
www.capstonepub.com

Books published by Capstone Press are manufactured with paper
containing at least 10 percent post-consumer waste.

Library of Congress Cataloging-in-Publication Data
Dunn, Mary R.
 Piranhas / by Mary R. Dunn.
    p. cm.—(Pebble plus. South american animals)
 Includes bibliographical references and index.
 Summary: "Simple text and photographs present piranhas, how they look, where they live, and what they do"—
Provided by publisher.
 ISBN 978-1-4296-7586-4 (library binding)
 1. Piranhas—Juvenile literature. I. Title. II. Series.
QL638.C5D86 2012
597'.48—dc23   2011027038

Editorial Credits
Katy Kudela, editor; Lori Bye, designer; Svetlana Zhurkin, media researcher; Kathy McColley, production specialist

Photo Credits
Alamy: Amazon Images, 7, Reinhard Dirscherl, 19; Corbis: John Madere, 13; Dreamstime: Magomed Magomedagaev,
5; Getty Images: Rodger Jackman, 15; National Geographic Stock: Joel Sartore, 21, Paul Zahl, 17; Shutterstock: Dmitrijs
Mihejevs, cover, 9, guentermanaus, 11, Photofish, 1

Note to Parents and Teachers

The South American Animals series supports national science standards related to life science.
This book describes and illustrates piranhas. The images support early readers in understanding
the text. The repetition of words and phrases helps early readers learn new words. This book
also introduces early readers to subject-specific vocabulary words, which are defined in the
Glossary section. Early readers may need assistance to read some words and to use the Table of
Contents, Glossary, Read More, Internet Sites, and Index sections of the book.

Printed in the United States of America in North Mankato, Minnesota.
102011   006405CGS12

Table of Contents

Amazon Swimmers

Piranhas prowl the warm
waters of South America.
They lurk among plants.
Swish! Hungry piranhas
dart out to catch a meal.

World Map

North
America

Europe

Asia

Africa

South
America

Australia

Antarctica

At least 20 kinds of piranhas

live in South America.

They live in creeks and ponds.

They swim in the muddy

Amazon River.

South America Map

where piranhas live

6

Up Close!

Most piranhas are small.

But some grow up to

2 feet (0.6 meter) long.

No matter their size, all

piranhas have shiny scales.

Piranhas have sharp teeth.

Chomp!

Piranhas snap their strong jaws

closed like a trap

to catch their food.

Finding Food

Piranhas are smart predators.

They hide near plants

to catch small fish and insects.

Some snatch young birds

that fall into the water.

Sniff! Sniff! Piranhas'
sense of smell leads them
to food. They find fruit
and small seeds floating
in the water.

Growing Up

A female piranha lays her eggs
near plants. The young fry
hatch in two to 10 days.
One or both parents
might guard the young.

fry

Piranha fry grow quickly.

A few days after hatching,

they go in search of food.

Some join schools.

Piranhas live up to 10 years.

Staying Safe

In the cloudy waters,

piranhas watch for predators.

People are a danger too.

Snip! Quick piranhas bite

fishing lines and swim free.

Glossary

Amazon River—the second-longest river in the world; it flows through South America

fry—baby fish

guard—to watch over and keep safe

hatch—to break out of an egg

jaw—a part of the mouth used to grab, bite, and chew

lurk—to lie hidden

predator—an animal that hunts other animals for food

prowl—to move around quietly and secretly

scale—one of the small pieces of hard skin covering the body of fish and reptiles

school—a large number of the same kind of fish swimming and feeding together

Read More

Berendes, Mary. *Piranhas.* New Naturebooks. Mankato, Minn.: Child's World, 2008.

Ganeri, Anita. *Piranha.* A Day in the Life: Rain Forest Animals. Chicago: Heinemann Library, 2011.

Jackson, Tom. *Piranhas and Other Small Deadly Creatures.* Crabtree Contact. New York: Crabtree Pub., 2009.

Internet Sites

FactHound offers a safe, fun way to find Internet sites related to this book. All of the sites on FactHound have been researched by our staff.

Here's all you do:

Visit *www.facthound.com*

Type in this code: 9781429675864

Super-cool stuff!

Check out projects, games and lots more at
www.capstonekids.com

Index

Word Count: 199

Grade: 1

Early-Intervention Level: 18